Weir's balance and proof measure system, for cutting oats, calculated to fit all variety of shapes, with unerring certainty ..

Robert [from old catalog] Weir

WEIR'S

BALANCE

AND

PROOF MEASURE SYSTEM,

FOR

CUTTING COATS,

CALCULATED TO FIT ALL VARIETY OF SHAPES,

WITH UNERRING CERTAINTY.

TRUTH can harm nobody, and therefore it is no injustice to others to say, that experience has decided, that this System, based on Proof Measures finding its own balance, is superior to anything yet published on Cutting Garments.

BOSTON:

PRINTED BY WILLIAM ELDER, 52 LEVERET STREET.

1855.

INTRODUCTION.

In every new undertaking of a public character, it is expected that the projector will offer some reasons for embarking in the enterprise; and more especially is this true in regard to publications, either intended to advocate old theories, or to introduce new ones. The multiplicity of books, charts, etc., for the advancement of useful knowledge, warrants the expectation, that the new author should, at least, briefly state his claims to popular attention. In the present case, it will appear the more proper, from the fact, that we are entering upon a somewhat trodden path.

Improvements in the mechanic arts, and inventions calculated to lessen the application of manual labor, are identified with the history of the present age. The practical effects which have resulted from this spirit of enterprise and improvement are to be witnessed in almost every department of operative industry, and have opened for the aspiring and ambitious new avenues to wealth and fame.

Every person who reviews the history of the past few years, can but recognize the rapid march of improvement, and the triumph of new truths in science and art, over old dogmas and a a long established course of error; antiquated customs have been shaken off, false theories have given way before the light of science, rude and uncouth mechanism has become fashioned by art—indeed "progress" has characterized all measures for the public good, and the arts have attained a degree of perfection which few of us could, twenty years ago, have anticipated.

Although the ordinary mechanical pursuits have in some instances been overlooked in the advancement of public enterprises of magnitude, still it is believed that in these departments of industry there is a field for useful and practical improvements, and it cannot be denied that, of late, some successful efforts have been made in the science of which the present work treats.

Much has been written and published of late years with a view of improving the art of cutting. Many systems have been proposed and adopted, and doubtless much benefit has been derived by their observance, but the sinister and injudicious policy which leads each projector of a system to extol his own, to the utter exclusion of others, tends very much to render all useless, from neglect, unless some work of a more prominent character than has yet appeared shall give them publicity, and the commendation they merit. Habit has indeed a most powerful influence upon the acceptance or rejection of theories; old prejudices are not easily removed. That there may be persons whose judgement is so discriminating, and whose conceptions are so clear, that they seldom miss their object, we are perfectly willing to allow, there is little probability that such persons will forsake their usual course to adopt a new one, and there is little need of such a change; but there are others less favored, who so pertinaciously adhere to past usages, that rather than submit to the guidance of any system for measuring and cutting, they will risk and endure the inconvenience and expense of making alterations. There is no gentleman who does not wish that his shall be a smooth and neat fitting garment, and none, who who is willing to pay for those which he is conscious have been spoiled by neglect, inattention or a bad system, the small sum paid out for a good system is money well invested.

Within fifteen or twenty years greater attention has perhaps been given to improvements in Cutting, than has been bestowed upon any other of the operative branches of industry. Systems have multiplied almost without number, and great anxiety for improvement has been evinced in the expenditures for these rules. It is well known to the profession, that, previous to the introduction of the "Third Rule," or the "Old Thirds," as commonly called, that Cutting was governed by no fixed principle whatever,

—this was the first attempt to apply the science of numbers, to the purpose of making diagrams for Cutting. This, the reader will understand, was a breast measure system. No sooner was it introduced, than it was found to be defective; there was, however, one very important point gained — there was data furnished from which inventive minds could reason, and it is from this point we date the extraordinary improvements that have marked the progress of our business.

The principles connected with the division of the measure, have been applied in more than a thousand different ways, still defects remain. The systems which have followed each other in rapid succession since, have been no more successful, yet some of the authors have pretended to reach the NE PLUS ULTRA; this has been done so frequently, that the man who would now present anything new upon the subject, would incur the risk of appearing ridiculous.

Neither the "Third Rule," or any other breast measure system, is a good guide to fitting, nor ever will be, until all mankind grow in one uniform shape. The trade has, notwithstanding, gained great benefit from certain systems, and they are worthy of preservation. Should every other revolution in the art be productive of as much good, we may hope to see the time, when the employment of "bushelmen" will be confined to repairing.

We have frequently met with inventors of rules, who, upon enquiry for an explanation of the various scales and divisions used by them in drafting, could give no other answer, than that such was the rule, and that they discovered its operation more by chance, than by any fixed principle, or sound reasoning. Such arbitrary and inexplicable rules, can be of but little utility. What would any intelligent man think of a system, published by such a person? He could but regard the production as trash, and the inventor as an imposter. No attempt seems to have been made to criticise these so called rules, in public, or by investigation, to expose the total lack of principles, upon which they are claimed to be established. It would be apparent to any unprejudiced mind, that they were "cabbaged," or made up of parts of other systems, published and sold to the unwary, as original inventions. Certainly this is not just, and the man who would knowingly lend his name as reference or endorsement of such publications, is undeserving of public confidence.

That the unnecessary multiplication of rules, is, in itself, an evil, every candid thinking man will admit. If every author or publisher were called upon, by way of introduction, to give a full and accurate explanation of the principles upon which his system is said to be based, it would tend to check the operations of those ignorant pretenders, who have overspread the country with a variety of rules and systems, which are not worth the paper upon which they are printed. The multiplicity of these valueless publications, or the prejudices of those who have suffered from the imposition of these "catch-pennys," have, through fear of being hoaxed a second time, declined to patronise any work, whether it should possess merit or otherwise.

We are not fanatical, or foolishly radical in our views, nor are we so stupidly conservative, as to repudiate all progress, as evil; we favor progress in the right direction,—that progress which promotes the public welfare. A few moments of observation in our public streets, will convince any person of taste and judgment, that the business of cutting, is not unfrequently conducted by persons wholly incompetent. Nothing can be more displeasing to the eye of taste, than the appearance of the miserable apologies for garments, which, in some cases, are worn by persons who are wholly unconscious that they possess any great defects. Let us endeavor to detect the lurkingplace of this mischief, and, if possible, expose it to the light, and by the combined wisdom of those who may wish to promote the respectability of the profession, a remedy may be pointed out.

GENERAL REMARKS.

Precepts and rules should be few, natural, and expressed with precision, and should occupy but a small space. In performing the service here called for, it is proposed to enter into a succinct review of the most popular of the systems that have been made public. A brief analysis only, will be presented, and the excellencies and defects of each pointed out. We shall, of course, be under some restraint, in regard to systems that are protected by copyrights, and intend to steer our course with regard to them all, so that no injury shall be sustained by their owners, in consequence of our labor, any further than candor and fidelity shall absolutely require. So far, however, as we differ in opinion, that difference shall be freely expressed, although we shall "nothing extenuate, or set down ought in malice."

The breast measure system, is the first in order, because it was the first introduced. This system is known by different names; it is called the mathematical rule, because the points of the draft are obtained by the combined calculations of division, addition, etc. The breast measure is made the basis of all the calculations. It now appears plain, that the basis of this rule is wrong, as applied to fitting the body, for whatever diversities may exist in the formation of a number of individuals, measuring the same around the chest, a third, a sixth, a twelfth, or a half, a fourth, or an eighth, will be the same in all cases, although each man may require variations peculiar to himself. It was originally assumed, that a third of half the breast measure, would give the right distance between certain points of a draft, that a fourth would give another, and so on. The man of mere figures followed the directions before him, and if he happened to fit well on the first trial, he, of course, pronounced the plan admirable; but some how or other, he found out that the plan did not work so well as at first supposed. This has led him to think that something is wrong. He will naturally ask what is the matter? The system cannot be any worse than when he purchased it; the fault, he will conclude, was in himself; he will try again. He will, perhaps, vary the plan, by which he could fit a good form, and attempt to make it applicable to fitting a bad form, but with no better success.

While in this perplexity, a man enters, with an improvement on the breast measure rule. This is the very thing he wanted. He takes the improvement, and goes to work with new spirits; but, alas, he has only changed the difficulty—the error still remains. In a word, the basis of this system is wrong, and no calculation or deduction can make it right.

The shoulder measure, as adopted by Mr. Hearne, and used in connection with the breast, was an improvement in the right direction, but still subject to a few of the difficulties attending the breast measure. Subsequently other shoulder measures were added, and systematized by Mr. Madison, and others, by which it has arrived at a certain degree of perfection, which warrants another attempt to remove all difficulties attending it. We have at present, more than a hundred different systems before us; nearly all of them belong to the same family, that is, THE BREAST MEASURE FOR BASIS. And our remarks are equally applicable to all.

There is another class of systems in use, which claims our attention, and deserves a passing notice. This class of rules differs in every particular from the last mentioned. It is founded on the actual measuring principle, by some, called the harness system, with buckle and strap attached; this is a method of taking measures by means of a strap of leather, or steel, passed around the body, under the arms, and fastened with a buckle, and from certain pivots in front, and back, the distance to all the various parts of the body are ascertained. This method claims originality and accuracy, in all its measures, and unerring certainty in transferring the measure taken to the cloth. As for the truth of the statement, we leave it to those who have used the rule, to decide. The majority of those with whom we have conversed on the subject, say, that it is very troublesome to the cutter, and annoying to the customer ; the measures are complicated, and will not, when applied to the cloth, give to a certainty that for which they were intended. For our part, we think of this method, that it is very good, when in the hands of an intelligent, practical cutter,—otherwise, it will increase the too prevalent practice, of employieg bushelling men.

We now proceed to set forth the improvements and advantages of this system, over all preceding ones.

In the prosecution of the task in which we have been engaged, three things were necessary ; first, to produce a set of measures, which would ascertain the various points of a coat, otherwise there would be no accuracy. Secondly, that the same measures would indicate in what position the person stood. Thirdly, to systematize those measures, so as to fit all variety of shapes and forms, according to the measures taken.

These objects are attained, and we are satisfied with the results. The measure are neither numerous nor complicated, being those measures that cutters generally apply, to find if the draft is correct, and called proof measures ; this being the case, why not make those proof measures the basis for building an unerring system upon.

1. From the top of the back, to the full length of waist, say 18 inches.

2. From the top of the back, passing the measure in front of the arm, and continuing to the full length of waist, 26 inches,—this is the balance measure. The difference between these two measures, is 8 inches, which is called the balance. By the balance, we ascertain the position in which the person stands, whether stooped or straight ; if stooped, the difference will be less, and if straight, the difference will be more. This balance, we claim as original, and will protect it.

3. Blade measure.

4. Upper shoulder measure.

5. Lower shoulder measure.

The three last-named measures are systematized, so as to fit any form or shape. By strictly following the dictates of this theory, the cutter will be certain of a good fitting coat, without trying it on, before finished. This, we believe, is a common practice with some cutters.

What a depravity of genius in the nineteenth century, when every art is striving for the mastery! There is no situation more awkward, than that of a cutter, who has mutilated his employer's cloth, which will frequently be the case, when a man has nothing but the poor resource of chance, or hope, that his work will fit.

It is a fact, that many employers have clothes thrown upon their hands, to a considerable amount, besides what they may have disposed of, by alterations. Such circumstances as these, must ever happen, while people are content to remain in ignorance. To be uninformed, may be the lot of many, whose inexperience has not furnished them with opportunities to compass the matter in question. True genius is not the lot of every one; yet almost every man is sufficiently enabled, by application and perseverance in certain rudiments, to acquire such a knowledge in any common manufacturing business, as will answer the practice of it. Some tailors sit down in the forlorn hope of struggling through, without ever enquiring further than the maxims of his father, or the erroneous principles of some antiquated breast measure rule. Such poverty of genius has always inhabited the minds of some men; or they never would have continued so long in such egregious errors! which have been handed down from father to son. One of the first things to be acquired, in order to the improvement of arts, and the enlarging of our ideas, is for a time to step out of the beaten way of common practice, and by a prudent reserve, make strict and judicious enquiries into the matter you would investigate, before you make any anti-conclusions to the theme in question. We are not unapprized of the objections which may be made to the bold assertion of arriving at perfection in any art.

We must confess, our best knowledge is sometimes imperfect and fallacious; after all our confidence, it is possible, things may be otherwise; this must be the case, when demonstrations are raised from false principles; but when genuine effects are produced, and proportionate systems appear from efficient causes; and when the object is within the boundaries of our intellects, we must pronounce the axiom incontrovertible.

The positive assertions of hypothesis, we own, may be alleged to be full of difficulty and doubt, especially in the art of cutting garments when the least error of appropriating or uniting the most trifling separation of any of the parts, would tend to produce a misfitting garment. This we may admit, but this could not happen where the practice is coincident with the theory. We hope our maxims will be universal; that every one may know and practice them: study the principle of each measure, and how it is applied on the draft, to correspond with the part over which the measure passes: when these things are attained, the draft can be executed with ease and satisfaction.

MEASUREMENT.

The order of the measures as taken, are as follows :—

1. Before you request your customer to take off his coat, place your measure at the top of the back, and find the full length of the waist, say 18in. ; continue to full length of skirt. This measure is taken over the coat, in order to find the length of waist accurately. You will now request your customer to take off his coat, make a mark between the shoulder blades, say 8 1-2 inches from the top of the back ; then place your measure at the top of the back, as before, and measure to the full length of waist, 18 in. ; make a mark at this place.

2. Still holding the measure under the thumb of the left hand, at the top of the back, pass it round in front of the arm, and find the distance to the length of waist at 18in. ; say 26 inches.

3. Pass the measure close under the arm, and over the most prominent part of the shoulder blade, to the mark 8½, say 22 inches.

4. Carry the measure up to the top of the back, at the place of beginning, say 25 inches.

5. Now drop the measure down the centre of the back, about 4 or 5 in. between the back scyes, and pass it around in front of the arm, and back to place of beginning, say 25½ inches.

6. The length of sleeve, 33 inches.

7. Around the breast.

8, Around the waist.

All those measures are taken tight, except the balance measure.

RECAPITULATION.

To the mark between the shoulder blades, 8½.
To natural length of waist, 16.
To full length of waist, 18.
To full length of coat, 37.
Balance measure, 26.
Blade measure, 22.
Upper shoulder measure,25.
Lower shoulder measure, 25 1-2.
Length of sleeve to elbow, 20.
Full length of sleeve, 33.
Breast, 36. Waist, 30.

Measures as recorded in the Measure Book.—8½, 18, 37, 26, 22, 25, 25½ 20, 33, 36, 30.

The sleeves are now worn so large, that we do not deem it necessary to give any measure for them.

BALANCE.

To find the balance, subtract the full length of the waist from the balance measure, thus—

Balance Measure,	26
Length of waist,	18
Balance,	8

Whatever the difference between these two measures may be, a corresponding number will be found, on the end of the ruler, marked balance;—this gives the position of the shoulder. There is another balance in connection with this, which governs the distance; from A to 1, on the back, see Plate 1, Diagram 1.

It is well known to every intelligent cutter, that the upper shoulder measure of two persons, one straight and the other stooped, may be the same. If a certain division of the upper shoulder measure is taken, to find the distance from A to 1, on the back, it will remain the same in all cases. The result is a crease, or wrinkle in the neck of the coat, which will extend over the shoulder to the front of the scye, when on a straight man. And if the person is stooped, the coat will stand off from the neck. To remedy this defect, Scale 1, on the rule, has been so arranged, as to correspond to a balance of 6 inches, and for every inch, balance more than 6; deduct one quarter in drafting the back; (in Scale No. 1, each number is divided into 4 quarters.) And to every inch, balance less than 6, add one quarter, in all other parts of the draft, Scale 1, will be used as it is.

DRAFTING.

PLATE I. DIAGRAM 1.

The figures on the diagram, represent the number of the scale to be used

From A to 1, is Scale 1, upper shoulder measure.
From 1 to 3, is Scale 3, " " "
From 1 to 2, is Scale 2, lower shoulder measure, add ½ inch at 2.
16 inches is the natural length of the waist, square from line C. 18 in. is the full length of waist, square from the outside line.

PLATE I. DIAGRAM 2.

Place the back as represented, and mark the side seam.
From 3 to line G, is the blade measure, 22, Scale 1.
From 16 to line G, is 1-2 the waist, draw the line G.
Place the balance end of the ruler, square with the line G, so that the side of the ruler will range with point 2 on the back. Then mark at O, the balance 8 ; draw the line B, by O and 2. See the position of the ruler on Plate 3, Diagram 6.
From O to B, is Scale 1, lower shoulder measure.
From O to 3, is Scale 3, lower shoulder measure.
From 3 on the back, to e, is ½ the breast measure. Add ⅛ of breast.
From B to A, is Scale 4, upper shoulder measure.
From A to 5, is Scale 5, " " " See the position of ruler, on Plate 3, Diagram 7.
From e to F, is Scale 5, " " Add ¼in. at F, and ½in. front.
From B to 1, is Scale 1, lower shoulder measure.
From 1 to 2, on line D, is Scale 2, lower shoulder measure. Square the line D.
From 3 to 2, is Scale 2, " " " Square line H.
From 0 to 6, on line g, is Scale 6, upper shoulder measure.
From 0 to 7, is Scale 7, lower shoulder measure. This point is half way between line B and G.
From 0 to 6, is Scale 6, lower shoulder measure.
From 6 to 2 on the back, is Scale 7. Square to i. See Plate 3, Diag. 7.
Place your finger on the prominent part of the side seam, and bring point 2 on line i, and mark the side seam as represented. Now place the top of the back at a, and bring point 2 on line D. Mark the shoulder seam and gorge, by 5 to F.
Again, bring point 2 on line H, and mark out the scye, by the points 6, 3, 7 and 6. Cut the under part of the scye a ¼ of an inch below 6.
From 16 to 18, on the forepart, is the same distance as from 16 to 18, on the side seam. From 16 on the back, to 16 on the forepart, is ½ the waist measure, Scale 1. Square the line 18, and draw the line m by the diagonal line A, on the ruler.

PLATE I.

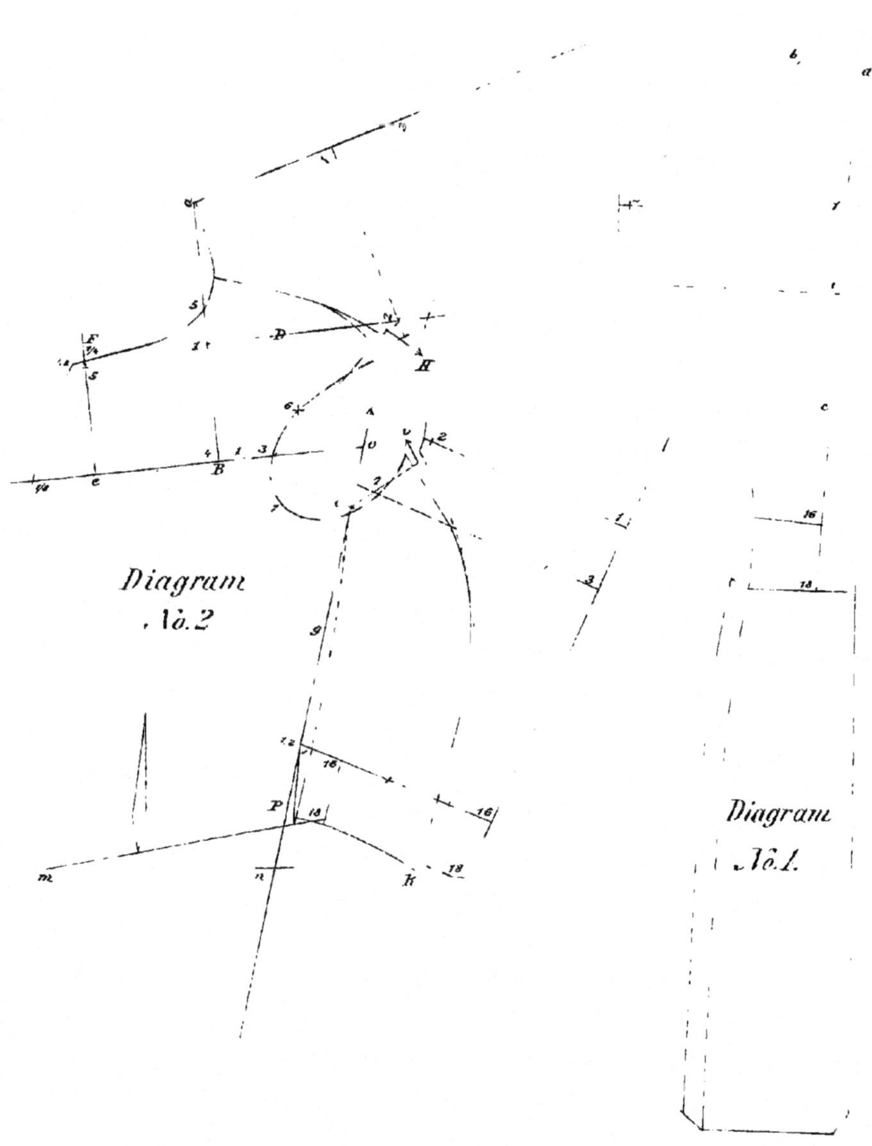

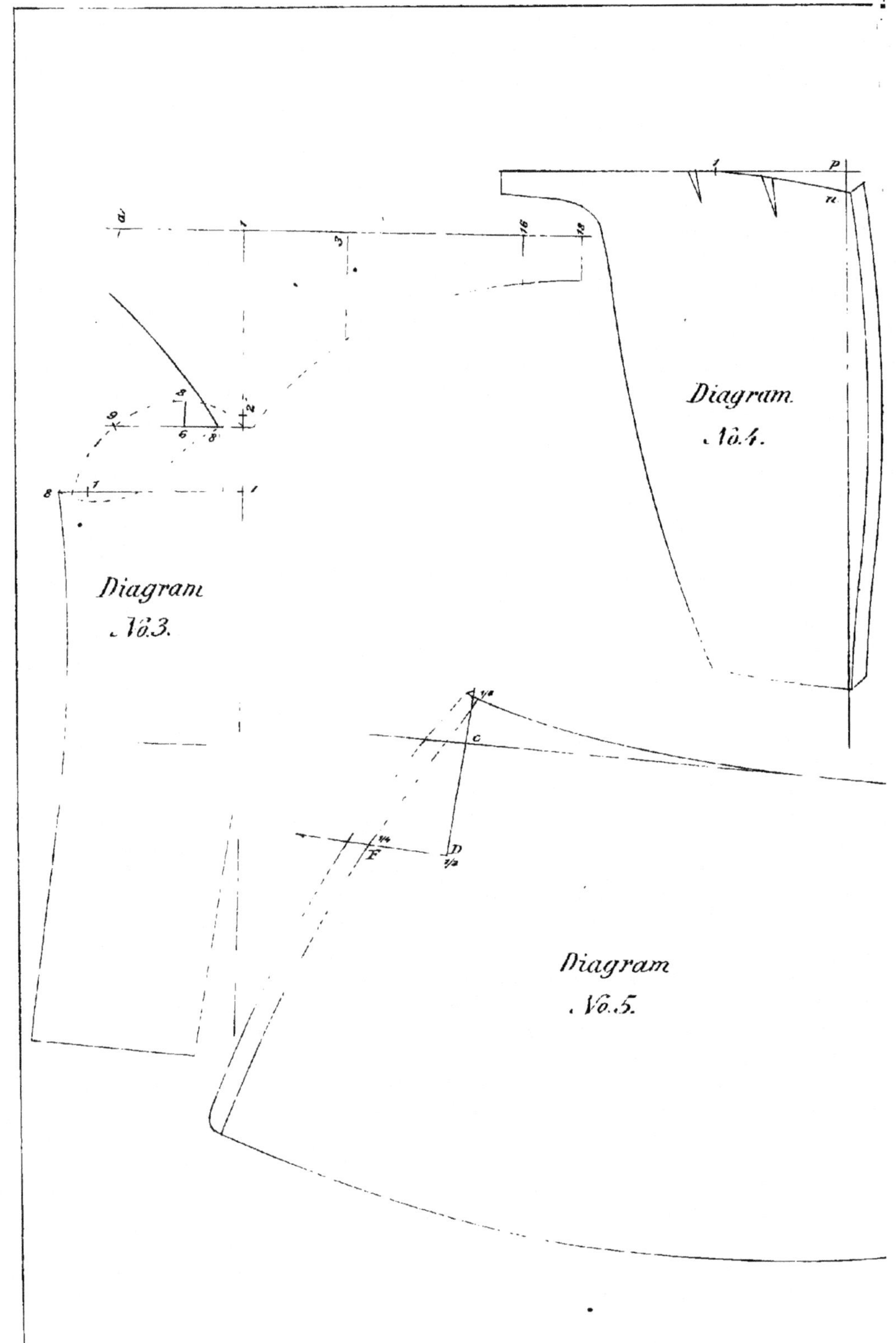
Diagram No. 3.
Diagram No. 4.
Diagram No. 5.

PLATE II. DIAGRAM 3.

When the forepart is cut, measure the scye, and draft the sleeve top by the scye measure, say 16 inches.

From 1 to 1, is the whole lower shoulder measure, Scale 1.

From 1 to 1, on the sleeve, is Scale 1, scye measure.

From 1 to 8, is Scale 8.

From line 2 to 6, is Scale 6, lower shoulder measure.

From 2 to 9, is Scale 9, scye measure.

From 6 to 8, is Scale 8. All other parts of the sleeve will be governed by measure or fashion.

From 2 to 8, under side sleeve, is Scale 8, scye measure.

PLATE II. DIAGRAM 4.

Draw a straight line n, and square to 1.

From P to N, is the same distance as from P to n, on Plate I, Diagram 2.

From P to 1, is Scale 1, ½ waist measure.

Form the skirt according to fashion.

The distance between those two points, P and n, on Plate I, Diagram 2, is obtained by drawing a line from point R to m. See Plate 1, Diagram 2. This distance will always give the proper spring for a skirt.

PLATE II. DIAGRAM 5.

Square from the front line to c, and draft by the breast measure.

From c to top, is ⅛.

From c to D, is ⅓.

From D to F, is ¼.

PLATE III.

Diagram No. 6.

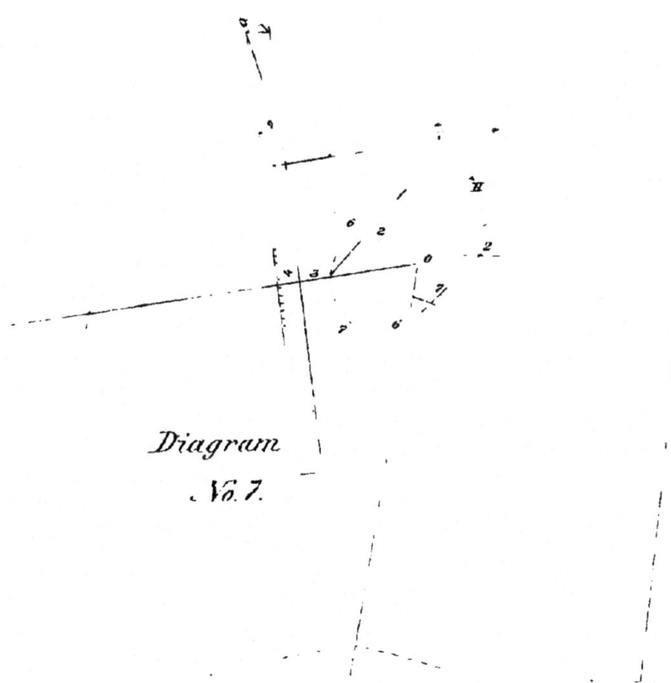

Diagram No. 7.

Diagram
No. 8.

Hip measure

PLATE IV. DIAGRAM 8.

This diagram is drafted same as Diagram 2, Plate 1, except the waist, which is drafted by the hip measure.

From 18 to line g, is ½ the hip measure.

From line g to m, is ½ the hip measure.

Add ¼ at m, as per diagram. Add lapel, and form the forepart.

From C to D, is ⅓ the hip measure.

From D to F, is 1-6 the hip measure.

CPSIA information can be obtained
at www.ICGtesting.com
Printed in the USA
LVOW03s1329090816
499654LV00018B/368/P